IT'S OUR REPUBLIC IF
WE ARE ALLOWED TO KEEP IT

A PRESERVATIVE, NOT A CONSERVATIVE

D.J. MAURO

Preface

"The Federalist Papers are the most important work in political science that has ever been written or likely ever to be written in the United States. It is, indeed the one product of the American mind that is rightly counted among the classic of Political theory and study.

This work has always commanded widespread respect as the first and still most authoritative commentary on the Constitution of the United States. It has been searched minutely by lawyers for its analysis of the powers of Congress. Quoted confidently by historians of the Constitution and cited magisterially by the supreme Court for its arguments in behalf of Judicial Review, Executive independent and national supremacy. To say the Federalist Paper stands third only the Declaration of Independent and the Constitution itself, among all the sacred writings of American political history.

The Revolutionary Background?

Anyone interest in thought, must read this Anti-Federalist. The United states during 1770 to 1784 is perhaps the most exciting period in any country's history. In the year 1773, as tension increased between the British colony. The king imposed a tax on tea. In 1773, "The Tea Party' was formed. The start of the Americans against taxation of something the colonists didn't want or needed. Each colony was more or less self-run government under its own state constitutions. But the officials of the monarch were three thousand miles away. The relationship became unsatisfactory and the separation with a Declaration of Independence ensued and the powers of the authority changed to Democracy. A new world of Democracy was at hand.

But the new nation was not a democracy. It was a constitutional representative republic. Our <u>framers</u> knew about democracies. That by one vote of the majority of the people could vote themselves anything they would want or even accept another system.

So welcome to the Republic and not a social democracy as did all the others after 1787.

Introduction

My name is D.J. Mauro. I was baptized Dominico, Jackamo, Geovoni, Christopher Colombo Mauro in a Catholic Church. I will be 92 in a few months. I've been married 71 years; have three children, boy girl twins and another boy now in their sixties. I can't believe my children are old enough to collect SSI. After high school, I received a working scholarship to Chouinard Art institute for two years and I met the one. I worked for two big electric utilities in California. I was a grunt, lineman, foreman, estimator, and a company rep. I am a working man like you.

I went to war to protect our Freedom in the Chinese Korean War, a United Nation War. Vietnam was another United Nation War, 50k killed. Then 5k here and there, for what? So, our children could learn about communism but now the young want socialism. Where did they learn that? Spell this out for yourself? The USSR-N.S.D.A.P. look in a dictionary.[95]

I ran for office in 1974 when Nixon, Kissinger and D. Rockefeller went to china under O.P.I.C. to move our economic future to third world. China, India, Mexico, others. Look to see where it's made? Newt Gingrich said we would have a service economy supplying technology. We got Bush I and II, Ford, Johnson, Clinton, and Obama. With 30 hours part time work without benefits. Remember before 2017, if you are still awake and thinking?

I didn't read the Federalist Papers or the Anti-Federalist papers until 2002 when I joined the Constitution Party. I said to myself "in Jesus Christ name." why isn't the book in our school and Sunday schools. How are we to love something we know nothing about. So, this is a cliff note of what are the warnings of today's social, political, economic problems spelled out in plain English. Now! Lookup factions in your dictionary, read it. Who are the false negatives and positives? Is there an answer for the economy?

Accreditation

I want to give the most wonderful women that have helped me decipher my ancient hieroglyphic tablets with strange language on them. Did he mean this, or the other way and they typed, read me as though they knew me before they met me. What a blessing and thank you to Teri, Pia, for their typing, extraordinary women, and Lin. Little 5 foot Jesus person and she introduced me to Jesus people and teachers of the Old Testament and invited Lin to meet my group The Tea Party. She was a little spit fire asking some question. Then Lin discovered what I was doing and read my manuscript. Lin had another new vision. Lin had never read anything like what our Founders wrote down for us. Lin introduced me to Sean. A black Jesus person. He liked what I wrote and took it with him. But he made me surrender like I never did before so now we are in the process of putting my work into a pamphlet or book and see if it is accepted. But there is one more person. Jan what striking beautiful woman. She was a Jesus person like Lin and if I needed typing done quickly, she would help. That's been my life for the last few months, and we shall find due in the next few months.

As it is written in the Anti-Fed Papers, "The manners, sentiments and interest of the people should be similar."

Thank you ladies and gentlemen, anyone would be very fortunate enough to have any of them for partner.

It's A Republic If We Are Allowed to Keep It

I would like to thank my beautiful wife of 71 years for the many months that I spent with four women putting everything into some order so it's understandable. She trusted me every time I was on the phone or away for a short time, she is one of the ones we all look for. Thank You Jesus!

It's A Republic If We Are Allowed to Keep It

Table of Contents

Chapter   **Page**

DONT TREAD ON ME

What Destroys Good Societies

The world was radically transformed during the 300-year period, from 1492 to 1787. During this time, explorers divided the globe into latitude and longitude. Regardless of the direction you travelled in this time, north or south, you encountered ice. The circumference of the globe was 24,000 miles on which, both Captain Cook and Magellan, discovered lands previously unknown.

Fast-forward, if you will to the 1780's. The United States is just thirteen states, scattered very far apart. Our Founding Fathers were painfully aware of the logistical difficulties this presented. In fact, it too days to get to Philadelphia, the first Capitol, for any meetings of importance. The distance from Maine, then part of Massachusetts, to Georgia was approximately 913 miles. From the Atlantic Ocean to the Mississippi River was approximately 750 miles. This area, and the thirteen states organized under it, formed our fledgling nation.

At the Philadelphia Convention in 1787, James Wilson stated in *The Anti-Federalist Papers*, "This jealousy misled the British with regard to America. The fatal maxims espoused by her were that the colonies were growing too fast, and that their growth must be stinted in time". [1] James Wilson introduced a new national idea on the floor of the constitutional convention. It was the 8th of October 1787 and with the statement, "I am bold to assert that it is the best form of government which has ever been offered to the world" *The Anti-Federalist Papers* were presented to our young nation.[2]

At the time of this introduction, monarchies, kings, or nobles ruled European countries. This resulted in a single person or family retaining the country's power. A single leader governed Spain, Portugal, and France. Nations in the "old world" organized colonies in Africa, Morocco, North, West and Southwest Africa, China, Hong Kong, India, and the West Indies.

Both *The Federalist* and *The Anti-Federalist Papers* warned of the dangers and difficulties of colonization. Governor Morris stated, in *The*

Anti-Federalist Papers, "The rich will strive to establish their dominion and enslave the rest. They always did. They always will". [3]

Three men began write articles in the colonist newspaper, *Publius,* explaining their ideas on the new nation to colonists. They were James Madison, who became our fourth president, John Jay, who became a Supreme Court justice, and Alexander Hamilton, who became our first Secretary of the Treasury.

Together these articles can be seen as a kind of instruction manual. They are as relevant today as they were in the 1780s, yet most Americans are unaware of both *Papers.* We do not, but should, teach this book in our schools, governments, and churches. Perhaps they were taught at one time. With the U.S. Literacy Rate at 99%, the absorption of these writings could reach an audience of millions.[4] Yet, despite a literacy rate of only 60% in 1787, most colonists were aware of *The Papers.*[5]

After reading *The Papers*, a single phrase has remained in my memory. In *Publius #78,* Alexander Hamilton wrote:

> that men acting by virtue of powers may not do only what their powers do not authorize, but what they forbid…or, in other words, the Constitution ought to be preferred to the statute, the intention of the people to the intention of their agents. [6]

This statement goes to the tenor of the statutes being introduced to Congress. This applies for all officers of the government that we the people elect. In between the lines there is a warning to the colonists and it remains true, to lay with the silent majority, is like playing dead to see what kind of funeral you have.

Why do we have a Republic and not a Democracy? In *Publius #39*, James Madison wrote:

> We may define a republic to be, or at least bestow that name on, a government which derives all its powers directly or indirectly from the great body of the people, and administered by persons holding their offices during pleasure for a limited period, or during good behavior. [7]

Madison goes on to say:

> It is essential to such a government that it be derived from the great body of the society, not from an inconsiderable portion or a favored class of it; otherwise a handful of tyrannical nobles, exercising their oppressions by a delegation of their powers, might aspire to the rank of republicans and claim for their government the honorable title of republic. [8]

By those standards, the Republics of today are Russia, China, Iran, and Iraq, to name a few. These *Publius* were meant as fact-based warnings.

The first part of *The Federalist Papers* addresses the weakness of the *Articles of Confederation*. The genesis of The Constitutional Representative Republic in 1787 was a letter written to George

Washington by James Madison on April 16, 1787. Although this letter is not included in the first *Federalist Papers* it is included in *The Anti-Federalist Papers*. In it Madison explains, that with thirteen individual independent nations or states, there is no unified defense, taxation, or order. He proposes that the states must become a union with a written constitution. That this union should have fixed laws, equality, justice, freedom, and happiness. With this a new concept of government was proposed.

Publius #8, written by Alexander Hamilton makes clear that the Articles of Confederation were weak, but the creation of a union would position the colonies adventitiously. Hamilton writes:

> If we are wise enough to preserve the union. Usually, we may enjoy the advantage of an insulated situation for a long time. Europe is a great distance from us. Her colonies in our vicinity will probably continue having such disproportionate strength to ours that they'll be unable to be a dangerous annoyance. Therefore, extensive military establishment will be unnecessary for our security. But if we become disunited, with the parts either separated or thrown together in two or three confederacies, in a short time we would be in the predicament of the continental powers of Europe. Our liberties would be at risk because of the armies needed to defend ourselves and against the ambition and jealousies of each other's. [9]

It's A Republic If We Are Allowed to Keep It

In 1787, the states united. *Publius #1* through #10 discuss various points furthering proof for the need of a union. The meat of *The Federalist Papers* begins with *Publius #10* with the word "factions". This word has significance both in *The Papers* and in our present-day world. The relentless bombardment of images tailored specifically to your interests, through various outlets, including the ever-present channels of social media, recalls the warnings of Orwell's *1984*. The phrase, "Be aware of the images" in the book warns us especially today to be conscious of our content consumption. After all, this is the way our information becomes public, the "factions" target us with their messages, we become subliminally controlled, and "zombified". If we are told a story enough times, we begin to believe it. This is what is happing as the "factions" vie for our mental space. Thus, we can no longer distinguish a lie from the truth. We are fed misinformation constantly. Most people cannot even tell you if our current government is a democracy or a republic. This is alarming, how can we know what to vote for and what we believe to be best for "we the people" if we don't know what kind of government we have.

Another word critical to our understanding of what our government was meant to be, is the word "we". Not all that long ago, the government was "we". It was not a fractious group of warring political parties splitting into shards of smaller political parties. This is yet another reason why all Americans should be well versed on *The Federalist Papers* and *The Anti-Federalist Papers*. Both the papers speak of factions, usurpations, corruption, cabals, treason, and tyranny. Not in theory, but in the sense of being prepared for a future inevitability. These were and are all warnings, and "we" must know what the warnings are. As a nation we are having trouble seeing them although they are all around us, silently influencing us, swaying us to one side or another relentlessly.

The factions and fractious nature of the U.S. are fat and happy, being fed by lies, untruths, diversity of passion, personal interest groups pumping negative information about candidates from both sides into our consciousness.

Hamilton writes about this very thing in *Publius* #68 stating:

But the convention have guarded against all danger of this sort with the most provident and judicious attention. They have not made the appointment of the President to depend on any pre-existing bodies of men who might be tampered with beforehand to prostitute their votes; but they have referred it in the first instance to the immediate act of the people of America...[10]

The answer you are looking for is, they didn't want parties making the decision for the chief magistrate of our new country.

When I finally looked up factions in the dictionary, I read this: "A group of citizens in an organization who have common interests, usually in opposition to the main principles or aims of the main body or nation;

contrary, hostile, opposed to"[11]

We all know people this could describe!

James Madison writes, in *Publius #10*:

> By a faction I understand a number of citizens whether amounting
> to a majority or a minority of the whole, who are united and
> actuated by some common impulse of passion, or of interest,
> adverse to the rights of other citizens, or to the permanent and
> aggregate interests of the community. [12]

The word "faction" deserves a careful examination in today's
political climate. The current "faction" is a disease that has destroyed
popular societies throughout history. The essential liberties must be
destroyed for a faction to exist; or give the faction what it wants. Article
IV Section 4 of our Constitution states: "The United States shall guarantee
to every State in this union a Republican Form of Government..."[13] At
this present time we have many factious organizations in the U.S.
Government that want democracy with socialism, not a constitutional
republic.

Publius #10 goes on to state:

> From this view of the subject it may be concluded that a pure
> democracy, by which I mean a society consisting of a small
> number of citizens, who assemble and administer the government
> in person, can admit of no cure for the mischief of factions. A

common passion or interest will, in almost every case, be felt by a majority of the whole; a communication and concert results from the form of government itself; and there is nothing to check the inducements to sacrifice the weaker party or an obnoxious individual. [14]

We see evidence of this happening on the television every day. *Publius #10* is of utmost importance. It continues:

Hence it is that such democracies have ever been spectacles of turbulence and contention; have ever been found incompatible with personal security or the rights of property; and in general, have been as short in their lives as they are violent in their deaths. Theoretic politicians, who have patronized this species of government, have erroneously supposed that by reducing mankind to a perfect equality in their political rights, they would at the same time be perfectly equalized and assimilated in their possessions, their opinions, and their passions. [15]

To this I'll add the "media", the fourth estate. Therefore, if all three powers are in unison, the fourth power is total tyranny!

Let's now look at the word democracy, which comes from the Greek word "demos", meaning common people, a majority, but is in essence mob rule. The word republic comes from the Latin word "public" meaning part of a whole; a portion of a whole; a large area, the entire portion unbroken whole. This describes the United States, a large area.

I must take a moment here to explain the fourth estate of our Republic. The fourth estate is the free press. It is the responsibility of the press to give us the truth, so you and I can make a proper judgment or discernment on something that will then affect our happiness, present, and future. If I write as a journalist and I leave something out, on purpose, that would be called deception. You would not get a clear, crystal clear, meaning to the story. So, what is truth? What is a lie? The tenor must be the truth of the information that you read for your discernment.

In the *Publius #2*, by John Jay, you will read the date 1773. The first Continental Congress September 1774. Which is the reason I wrote the above regarding fourth estate and the responsibility of the press and our centers of education is that was the day our revolution began. The Boston Tea Party took place in Massachusetts in 1773.

The people of America felt, correctly, that they were in imminent danger. They formed the Congress of 1774, which recommended certain measures that later proved prophetically wise. However, the immediate reaction by the press, including, pamphlets and weekly papers, warned against these measures as did many other quarters of the colonies. They relentlessly called to reject the advice of the patriotic congress. Many officers of the government obeyed the dictates of personal interest. Others predicted mistaken consequences, were unduly influenced by former attachments, or saw the dictates as a threat to ambitions that did not correspond with the public good, although men were deceived and decided judiciously. Reflecting back, they were happy they did so. That was the beginning of the United States of America and world democracy.[22]

If you tell a joke to a group, and leave out the punch line, no one will understand or laugh. The whole story is important and should be relayed to the people in complete form by journalists. Thus, the year 1774 is an important part of our education.

Let us now reflect on what we just read. In 1773, The Tea Party Rebellion started. Who had the power of the press? The English (British) government did. Moving forward to present day, to our present time, the 21st century, we see a country divided, just as we were in 1774. The difference is that the colonists lived in a country that was oppressive to them, a country that they were subjects to, under the authority of a King. Important to note here is that Britain was our first government.

On September 25, 2018, the President of the United States of America, a Republic and sovereign nation, spoke to the United Nations[91]specifically about the danger of socialism as a world movement; immigration as a world disaster due to gangs, drugs, slavery, and sex trafficking, and getting the United States out of the United Nations Human Rights Universal Declaration. Chaired by Eleanor Roosevelt (12/1948).

It's A Republic If We Are Allowed to Keep It

Articles 3-21- most countries of the world do not have a Constitution with our Bill of Rights as a guarantee of rights. But Articles 3-21 states that (page 102, Encyclopedia of the United Nations) "freedom of movement and residence – including everyone's right to leave any country; including his own". Well, you read the rest. I think President Trump has it together.

The United Nations was formed after World War II. The United States became a legal signatory in 1948. Alger Hiss was the first Secretary General Pro Tem of the United Nations.

Now do some homework. Read Article IV, Section 4 of our Constitution please. And Article VI of our Constitution. I am sure our present President has, or he would not have said what he did on the floor of World Government that day.

If we joined the United Nations, with a treaty, don't you think our Jackass or Elephant, would have said to you and I – "would you please pass a Constitutional Amendment to give up our Constitution for the new United Nations charter?" We need to be honest with ourselves; we are so close to a new world order, which will give us a new name, the United Socialist States of the Americas.

In 1954 Senator John W. Bricker of Ohio introduced an amendment to the United States Senate, to forbid these treaties to be made the supreme law of the land. The bill was called The Bricker Amendment, and failed by one vote; like President Obama's Health Bill, which failed by Senator John McCain's one vote. Most everyone knows nothing about the Bricker Bill. The only mention of the Senate having the power to make votes on treaties is in the *Anti-Federalist Papers*. The earliest *Papers* are by James Madison, pages 174-175:

> By declaring all treaties supreme laws of the land, the Executive and the Senate have, in many cases, an exclusive power of legislation; which might have been avoided by proper distinction with respects to treaties, and requiring the assent of the House of Representatives, where it could have been done with safety.[16]

The real danger is that only two/thirds vote would be present. Meaning, out of three Senators on the floor of the Senate, two Senators would have the power of the whole treaty for the whole nation. Think about that. Article 4, Section 4 and Article VI.

In *Publius #64*, John Jay writes regarding treatises:

> As to the corruption, the case is not supposable. He must either have been very unfortunate in his intercourse with the world, or possess a heart very susceptible to such impressions, who can think it probable that the President and two thirds of the Senate will ever be capable of such unworthy conduct. The idea is too gross and too invidious to be entertained. But in such a case, if it should ever happen, the treaty so obtained from us would, like all other fraudulent contracts, be null and void by the laws of nations.[17]

It's A Republic If We Are Allowed to Keep It

Now, 231 years after the grand awakening, we find ourselves at risk of losing our Constitution. What is the reason for this division - is this a Republic or a Democracy, or what? Have we been taken over by a minority faction of citizens, with some common passion or foreign interest, adverse to the Constitutional Republic? The warnings in almost every *Publius* are evident. But if this book, the *Federalist Papers*, is not in our schools or universities, there must be some secret cabal or society; some conspiracy, keeping this instruction manual from our children, and every one of us since the end of the Civil War.

DONT TREAD ON ME

Men of the Archives 1787

In the *Anti-Federalist Papers* we find that men are looking into the available archives of such universities as Harvard, in 1787. Harvard University, in Massachusetts Bay Colony, was established in 1636; Yale University in Princeton, New Jersey was established in 1746, Dartmouth College in New Hampshire was established in 1769, Columbia University in New York was established in 1754. William and Mary, Rutgers, and Brown were all established in 1787. Missionaries and men with Christian intent started every university mentioned above. The word virtue is not in our pulpits, or the halls of lawmakers or in our vocabulary any longer or used by factions.

It's A Republic If We Are Allowed to Keep It

Thomas Jefferson spoke about Plato's Republic. Recall the story of the cave, where people were chained to the wall unable to look to the right or left. All they knew were the shadows on the wall, walking behind them, from the light behind them. That was their only reality. When they were released from the wall, they could not believe what they saw. Their whole existence was those shadows on that wall. Yet when they walked out of the cave there was another reality. As things became normal, they could not forgive their captors from keeping the truth from them and hated them for it. That was the world before 1787.

Thomas Jefferson wrote of the book, in a letter to John Adams in July 1814:

> While wading thro' the whimsies, the puerilities [childishness], and unintelligible jargon of this work, I laid it down often to ask myself how it could have been that the world should have so long consented to give reputation to such nonsense as this? [18]

Plato's Republic was not a republic. Athens was a small city that controlled a vast amount of the known world; it was the seat of government, where the laws and measures were passed. The city of Athens advanced and was examined in the archives of Plato's Society. Their strange laws said that children belong to the State and that older men could live with young boys (elimination of marriage), much like today?

Plato lived for 80 years, from approximately 428 to 347 B.C to many he may have seemed to have his head in a cloud, considering that he was a philosopher of a utopia like Atlantis and underground caves. I agree with Thomas Jefferson. It was a lot of nonsense.

Other philosophers included Socrates (470 - 399 B.C.) and Aristotle (384 – 322 B.C.) – 62 years. Aristotle wrote,

> If the youth are not exposed to the principles on which our nation was based, they cannot be expected to love what they do not know. They can experience the personal freedom that we still to a degree retain, but they cannot know their own heritage if they are not exposed to it.

The men of our Constitutional Republic must have read Voltaire, Turgot, Rousseau, or Cicero – who knows what they read or researched? But we had better get reading and understand the foundation our government was based on before this republic form of government is taken from the face of the earth.

Over the years we have seen many factions. Apure democracy made up of a large whole would not work for a democratic government. It has to be a Republic; for a large land mass, a Constitutional representative Republic with written laws, just and fair; a free enterprise system. Where the people have the power and the people they put into office would support and defend the Constitution of the United States of America (as written). Where politicians would not be allowed to be office for twenty or thirty years; they are put in office for their good ideas, not for life. Any law or statute that does not support the Constitution should be null and void. *Publius #78* reads, "Men acting by virtue of power, may not only what their powers do not authorize, but what they forbid". [19]

It is my goal to put into the pamphlet as much as I can about important sections, of both the *Federalist* and *Anti-Federalist Papers* that have a special meaning. I hope you will understand the way I present both books to you. Jay, Madison, and Hamilton were at the Philadelphia Convention putting into words what they, and the rest of the men on the floor of the convention, were deciding for the new form of government.

The average reader may overlook that their opinions may not be like mine. However, the thoughts of these men, that put so much effort into creating this instruction book, are of utmost importance today.

Recall *Publius #10*, factions are a disease that has destroyed popular government throughout our history. Factions destroy within, just as they are doing today. This is a popular government to many of us, only if you read the instruction manual.

Alexander Hamilton states, in *Publius #78*:

There is no position, which depends on clearer principles, than that every act of a delegated authority contrary, contrary to the tenor of the commission under which it is exercised, is void. No legislative act, therefore, contrary to the Constitution can be valid. To deny this would be to affirm that the deputy is greater than his principal; that the servant is above his master; that the representative of the people are superior to the people themselves; that men acting by virtue of powers may do not only what their powers do not authorize, but what they forbid. If it be said that the legislative body are themselves the Constitutional judges of their own powers and that the construction they put upon them is conclusive upon the other departments it may be answered that this cannot be the natural presumption where it is not to be collected from any particular provision in the Constitution. It is not otherwise to be supposed that the Constitution could intend to enable the representatives of the people to substitute their will to that of their constituents.[20]

The Constitution is, in fact, and must be regarded by the judges as a fundamental law; a law is a rule of action. Any law or statute introduced on the floor of the House of Representatives or the Senate is automatically null and void. If the statute does not support the Constitution, you weaken the Constitution, because the Constitution must be preferred over the statute. If the constituents (citizens) elect lawmakers that have no idea what I just copied out of our instruction book, don't vote for them! "We the People" are superior to judges and the legislators. Judges must regulate their decisions by the fundamental law, rather than those that are arbitrary.

The Federalist Papers again make it very clear, as do The Anti-

Federalist Papers, about the qualifications of the people we appoint or elect to office to make decisions that affect our lives, security, and happiness. As it says in *Publius #78*:

> According to the plan of the convention, all judges who may be appointed by the United States are to hold their offices *during good behavior*; which is conformable to the most approved of the State Constitutions, and among the rest, to that of the State.[21]

That statement applies to all officers, or anyone we vote for; good behavior is the most important. Are they supporting the Constitution? If not, vote them out; they are a danger.

I remember reading in *The Anti-Federalist Papers* about some discussion having to do with a long-term residency requirement before immigrants would be allowed to vote. I also recall that before you could vote, you must have lived in your voting district for one year. Yet, all that changed with *Amendment 26*. The residency requirement was removed and the voting age changed from twenty-one to eighteen under the new amendment. The eighteen-year-old could vote without residency, because if the university or school he attended started in August or September the student was away from home he would not be eligible to vote. I'll let you think about the change in our country made at that time.

Today there is only a thirty-day residency requirement. So, if you have a home in New England and you have a winter home in Florida,

Southern Texas, or Arizona, you'd be able to vote twice. See how drastically a law can change the society without you realizing it? Read the rest of *The Federalist Papers*. Today the Democrats want the sixteen-year-old to vote. Know who controls our students; the education system. If these students' parents didn't get it…well, you get the point?

In an address President Alexander Hamilton, said in Publius 78,

The intentions of the people must be guarded over the intentions of their agent. This conclusion in no way means the judge is superior to the intent of the law as written in the statute. Judges must regulate their decisions by the fundamental law rather than by those that are not fundamental.[22]

Judges do not make laws!

You can have no feeling, understanding, or love for something you have never read or understood before. In a letter to James Madison from Paris on January 30, 1781,Thomas Jefferson wrote, "I hold it that a little rebellion now and then is a good thing, and as necessary in the political world as storms in the physical." [24] What this means is that we must read often, or be reminded, why this book is so important to how we are governed. Again, why is this book absent from our classrooms at every level?

In *Publius #51* James Madison writes:

It may be a reflection on human nature that such devices should be necessary to control the abuses of government. But what is government itself but the greatest of all reflections on human nature? If men were angels, no government would be necessary. If angels were to govern men, neither external nor internal controls on government would be necessary. In framing a government which is to be administered by men over men, the great difficulty lies in this: you must first enable the government to control the governed; and in the next place oblige it to control itself.[25]

If you like to read, read the entire *Publius #51*. It's good. I took some class units at a junior college on political science and the classics, like Steinbeck and the Brothers Karamazov (a novel by Fyodor Dostoyevsky). A very spiritual story. We were just about to read the *Grand Inquisitor* in the book when the professor said we were coming to the winter recess or Christmas and we would wait until we returned to discuss this reading. She wanted us to read it; take notes, write sentences, make a story of what we got out of it.

I read it three times and put my sentences together. The *Grand Inquisitor* was the tale of Ivan telling a story to Alyosha. To me, it was like Jefferson debating Karl Marx, or Jesus debating Lucifer. This is what I read before the class:

Our work has only begun. It has long to wait until completion and the earth has much to suffer, but we shall triumph and become

Caesars and then we shall plan the universal happiness of man. *"Receiving bread from us they will see clearly that we take bread made by their hands, from them, to give to them without any miracles."*[26] *Oh, we shall persuade them that they will only become free when they renounce their freedom to us and submit to us.* [26] They know the value of complete submission and until men know that they will not be happy. *"Oh, we shall allow them even sin, they are weak and helpless, and they will love us like children because we allow them to sin. We shall tell them that every sin will be expiated, if it is done with our permission, that we allow them to sin because we love them, and the punishment for these sins we take upon ourselves... And they will have no secrets from us.* [26] They must be deceived to be happy.

As I read and wrote what I read in Dostoyevsky's *The Grand Inquisitor*, I said to myself, "How many others have understood the nature of man?" As a young man, I read "Brave New World" by Aldous Huxley, published 1932. Yet another story on how man can be easily controlled by another. As it is written in James Madison's *Publius #51*, " men are not angels". [27] I remember reading about a witch doctor in Africa who found a tablet showing the moon cycles, eclipses of the sun and then the moon. There would be lots of power in his hands if he could make the moon and sun disappear. He could be a god, a great leader, and a great man. For good or evil, not from a small fraction of the society.

Now you just read a factious story about Ivan telling Aloysha a story of the universal happiness of man through deception, "taking bread made by their hand from them to give it to them without any miracles". [28]

The Internet can be used for good or evil. It is essential that a republic government spring up from the people now! Men are not angels? Sergey Nechayev (1847-1892) wrote a book called *The Revolutionary Catechism,* a very diabolical book at how to control the human race. So, maybe Adolf Hitler read it, or Karl Marx, Vladimir Lenin, or Napoleon? All these men were born in the age of revolution, in the 17th and 18th century. Most could have read the *Grand Inquisitor*. I am not supposing we all think the same, but some get an idea and run with it. Some are inspired by violence and hatred. There is a word for this and it is, factions. See *The Federalist Papers, Publius #10* by James Madison, below. We as a nation have never understood what is in it. The year 1774 was well into the age of revolution. Therefore, it's worth repeating again:

> AMONG the numerous advantages promised by a well-constructed Union, none deserves to be more accurately developed than its tendency to break and control the violence of faction. The friend of popular governments never finds himself so much alarmed for their character and fate, as when he contemplates their propensity to this dangerous vice. He will not fail, therefore, to set a due value on any plan which, without violating the principles to which he is attached, provides a proper cure for it. The instability, injustice,

and confusion introduced into the public councils, have, in truth, been the mortal diseases under which popular governments have everywhere perished; as they continue to be the favorite and fruitful topics from which the adversaries to liberty derive their most specious declamations. [29]

DONT TREAD ON ME

Changing Immigration Laws

Our republic is a popular government. We are witnessing factions, the Democratic (or Jackass) and the Republican (or Elephant) parties.

The Jackass Party lost to the Elephant party, and the plan of the new world order was almost in place when by a fluke in the original Constitution, The tenor of the Electoral College (which was to protect the smaller states) worked. The College of today is to work for the most populous states and Donald Trump, aka Donaldo Maximus, did the unthinkable and became President.

The Jackass Party, long waiting for completion, fizzled out, and the power cabal will not be Caesars, but we are in for a long time of suffering because the Jackass Party hates this Republic. Their plan was for democracy, and as Madison said in *Publius #10*, democracies are always full of contention and turbulence. Their lives are as short as their deaths are violent. Political theorists who support this type of government erroneously suppose that when people are reduced to a perfect political equality (like utopian socialism) their passions will also be equal. Their passions are loud as is their hate of others because of their own discomfort. Administering a socialist government won't cure the harm caused by the faction within the pure democratic government. A common passion or interest will almost always be felt by a majority of the whole. There is nothing to check the inducement to sacrifice the weaker party of obnoxious individuals.

In *Publius #48*, James Madison writes:

The conclusion which I am warranted in drawing from these observations is that the mere demarcation on parchment of the constitutional limits of the several departments is not a sufficient guard against those encroachments which lead to a tyrannical concentration of all the powers of government in the same hands.[30]

Note, there is a warning here. Again, look at the last hundred years of the Jackass and Elephant parties; maybe that is why these *Papers* are out of our churches and schools?

In *The Anti-Federalist Papers* it is written:

The manners, sentiments and interests of the people should be similar. If this is not the case there will be a constant clashing of opinions and the representatives of one part will be continually striving against those of the other. This will retard the operations of the government and prevent such conclusions as will promote public good.[31]

Today, as we strive more toward a democracy and not a republic political equality, let's look at the political equality of the socialist, like Karl Marx and Friedrich Engels. Engels was a wealthy industrialist in England who sponsored Marx in writing *The Communist Manifesto*. Let's have a clear understanding of proletariat and bourgeoisie. The proletariat was the lowest class under the Roman Society: slaves, workers, and bourgeoisie. A class between the aristocracy - moneyed and working class – both would be characterized as the world before the American Republic. Emperors, kings; aristocratic, oppressive, wealthy, subjects, property owned by the few – that was the world before 1787. The world was transformed from the power of one man or family rule, to a democracy of the people.

Most societies of the eighteenth through to the twenty-first century were democratically elected. Democracy is popular because people make decisions for themselves, but democratic societies are for small countries, like Switzerland where you don't need to go far to vote.

After more than two centuries, the Republic of America remains the oldest written national constitution in use in the world. Sadly, passing unconstitutional statutes that have sidestepped the tenor of the elected agents has weakened it. All this because, the "instruction manual" is not taught in our educational system. The original intent has changed so much that we have an oligarchy of two similar parties, and we are now favoring more socialism. If I read Marx and Engels correctly, we will end with the dictatorship of the proletariat, which was what we stopped in 1787.

Would you agree that manifesto puts us back to the old world, with the new brand of titans and unbelievably wealthy, which will oppress the working class again? If you keep reading this thesis of mine, somewhat however unbelievable that it would be; you will see that Dostoevsky is right. We humans are stupid enough to accept socialism; to be deceived to be happy. In this new world order of socialism, we have come full circle.

In the *Anti-Federalist Papers*, under the title Brutus, (New York lawyer), you will find his statement that, "The territory of the U.S. is a vast extent. It now contains near three million souls (in 1787) and is capable of containing much more than ten times that number". [32]

The United States census for 2000 was 248,421,906. [33] I bet the population is closer to 400 million at the present time because in 1965, President Lyndon B. Johnson signed bills called S500 and HR2580, passed October 3, 1965 – Public Law 89-236.[34] This bill was introduced by Senator Ted Kennedy, changing our legal immigration quota from 1924 of 250,000 legal immigrants – 85% percent from first world countries, which could read and write in their own language, and fifteen percent from third world countries who couldn't read or write.

Bill S500 and HR2580 changed to legal 250,000 to 900,000 to legal immigrants, 85% of that 900,000 now come from third world countries.[35] Most cannot read or write and are from authoritarian or dictator led countries. However, that is not the whole story. Once you get your citizenship, you are allowed to bring your families over to this land we love. Now, you can bring your mothers, fathers, brothers, sisters, uncles, aunts, nieces and nephews. This is your legal immigration system today – not including illegals. So, if married, both sides can bring their families.

Now, from 1965 to 2018 (53 years), take your calculator out and do the math – multiply 53 by 900,000, and say only half of the 900,000 (or even all) bring their families? That is what is called chain immigration.

The media has told you that there are only twenty million illegals in this country for the last 20 years. Do you really believe that? Is there something slipping by us? Who is telling you the truth, and who is lying?

Lewis & Clark told President Jefferson, when they can back from the Pacific coast, that there was room for 300 million people, and there would be enough to sufficiently provide for them without trouble. Today, we are in trouble! I bet most don't know who Lewis and Clark are?

DONT TREAD ON ME

Genesis of Illegal Immigration

During WWI, America sent their boys to fight in Europe. We contracted Mexican labor to harvest crops while our boys were in Europe. That program was called The Bracero Program. The war ended in 1918, but the Bracero Program was extended to 1922. Mexican workers who came to work totaled 76,862, but only 34,922 returned to Mexico.[36] Braceros were exempt from income tax and Supplemental Security Income (SSI). They continued to make more than United States citizens because they were exempt from income tax. This statute started the flow of illegals and the farmers didn't have to account for any of them. During WWII, the Bracero Program started again and continued through the Korean War. The Braceros were to work in agriculture only and were terminated in the early 1960s.

We also had a program of labor from the British West Indies, Jamaica, the Bahamas, St. Lucia, St. Vincent, Dominica, and Barbados. All English-speaking countries. We now have other programs, like H-1 Visas, HIA-Visas. Does all this sound insane? I thought these visas started in the 1990s. Everything you have read here comes from *State of Emergency* and *Death of the West* both by Pat Buchanan.

I lived in California at the time of Caesar Chavez, an American labor leader, who co-founded the National Farm Workers Union in 1962. There were two strikes, one in North California, and one in Central California. In the town of Watsonville, in Santa Cruz County, there was a phrase "the Mexican workers are tired and lonely for their families. So, why don't we bring their families here to help pick the crops and the men don't have to go to Mexico to see them". And what did the Jackass and Elephant do? Remember Publius #78, what is forbidden?

Remember *Publius #78*, "Men acting by virtue of power may not only do what their powers do not authorize, but what they forbid. The intention of the people must be guarded to the intention of their agents."[37]

Our Constitution has been weakened. "Men acting by virtue of power may not do what their powers do not authorize, but what they forbid" – say it and read over and over, it's that important.[38]

At about the same time, the second President Bush was meeting with President Vicente Fox of Mexico, and Prime Minister Steven Harper of Canada. They created what was called The Security and Prosperity Partnership (S.P.P.) or the North American Free Trade Agreement (N.A.F.T.A.). It would start a new union, like the one in Europe, without a constitutional amendment. The first President Bush talked about a new world order at a State of the Union. Goods, capital, and people would move across our borders north and south. Mexico would move north and stay! But, could Americans go to Mexico to work and vote?

In *Publius #47* James Madison writes:

The accumulation of all powers, legislative, executive, and judiciary, in the same hands, whether of one, a few, or many, and whether hereditary, self-appointed, or elective, may justly be pronounced the very definition of tyranny. There can be no liberty where the executive and legislative powers are united in the same person. The fundamental principles of a free constitution are subverted."[39]. Self-appointed are the bureaucracy in the deep state.

I don't think we are at the point of a military takeover by the current President, but I think the Party that replaces the elephant has already transformed the people to accept another "ism"; rather than the Constitutional Republic of the past, and that "ism" is socialism!

Many authors have published on how the United States is "non-extinction" or "non-extincting". There is a story in my notes about the Last Supper, with Jesus saying to the disciples: "This is my body, which is given for you. Do this in remembrance of me." [40] Jesus knew His time was short. Leaving the room, He said to the Disciples, "Hereafter I will not talk much with you: for the prince of this world cometh, and hath nothing in me." [41] That warning was about Lucifer.

If you think what you just read follows a pattern of some design to change or replace our Constitution, you may want to read some of the warnings that are in *The Federalist Papers*. They are the same warnings a President gave us, as he left office. I don't think that we are at that point with "Donaldo Maximus", but I think the party that replaces this President may be.

In *Publius #46 – The Influence of the State and Federal Governments Compared,* by James Madison, he wrote:

> The reasoning contained in these papers must have been employed to little purpose indeed, if it could be necessary now to disprove the reality of this danger. That the people and the States should, for a sufficient period of time, elect an uninterrupted succession of means ready to betray both; that the traitors should, throughout this period, uniformly and systematically pursue some fixed plan for the extension of the military establishment; that the governments and the people of the States should silently and patiently behold

the gathering storm and continue to supply the materials until it should be prepared to burst on their own heads must appear to everyone more like the incoherent dreams of a delirious jealousy, or the misjudged exaggerations of a counterfeit zeal, than like the sober apprehensions of genuine patriotism.[42]

In my very young life, one President gave a warning about the "military industrial establishment". It was President Dwight D. Eisenhower in 1961. Many have given us warnings from time to time. Maybe they know something or are prophetic, like the men who wrote the Federalist Papers? President Eisenhower, meaning to be prepared.

President John F. Kennedy, in a speech before November 22, 1963, said:

The very word secrecy in an open and free society is repugnant; honest people are opposed to secret societies and secret proceedings. For we are opposed historically and inherently around the world by a monolithic and ruthless conspiracy that relies on covert means for expanding its influence; on infiltration instead of invasion; on intimidation instead of free choice. It is a system that has concentrated vast amounts of human resources and material resources, into a tightly knit, highly effective machine, that combines military, diplomatic, intelligence, economic, scientific, and political operations. Its premeditations are concealed, not published; its defenders are silent. No secrets revealed. That is why the Athenian lawmaker, Solan, made it a crime not to tell the truth. That is why I am asking the American people for their help. I am confident, with your help, we can live free and independent.[43]

So read the book! It's the chance we have to save this Constitutional Representative Republic. If every, or most, countries on this spaceship called Earth would have something like our Constitutional Republic, we would be a lot better off in my opinion.

Alexander Hamilton, in his *Publius #60 – The Same Subject Continued,* states:

But what is to be the object of this capricious partiality in the national councils? Is it to be exercised in discrimination between the different departments of industry, or between the different kinds of property, or between different degrees of property? Will it lean in favor of the landed interest, or the moneyed interest, or the mercantile interest or the manufacturing interest? Or, to speak in the fashionable language of the adversaries to the Constitution, will it court the elevation of the 'wealthy and the well-born', to the exclusion and debasement of all the rest of the society?[44]

That is THE question? Not a question. If the above isn't clear by now, remember the *Grand Inquisitor*. We shall be Caesars, and the plan?

The universal happiness of man.

As Governor Morris said in *The Anti-Federalist Papers*, "The rich will strive to establish their dominion and enslave the rest. They always did. They always will".[45] And when we get to the whole point of what he

said, you'll be astonished, when you get to Publius #30 and #36, you will be surprised by the solution, a 25-cent chip.

We are sort of in a matrix today, but we are easily deceived, without noticing what movies (which are a form of faction) have already done to us. We have "taken" the pills (the red or the blue pill), and we see how far down the rabbit hole we have gone. The last three or four months have proven how deep into the rabbit hole we are with the faction that is prejudiced against our Constitutional Supreme Court then - appointee, Justice Brett Kavanagh. This is the lowest level of the rabbit hole. Like James Madison said in *Publius#10*, our instruction manual, factions have destroyed every popular society throughout history. "Their passions are loud and disruptive, and they hate others for their discomfort. Their lives are short as their deaths are violent." [46]

Democracy is known as mob rule. Whoever made the decision for the red and blue pill knew what they were doing. They, whoever they are, should have made the Democratic party the red party. Red is more in line of socialism than the blue pill; the flag of China and Russia were red at one time.

There is a story about the payment of taxes in the Bible most of us are familiar with. The Pharisees were trying to trick Jesus regarding the payment of taxes to whom? The Pharisees asked, "Whose face is on the coin?" The crowd yelled out "the Emperor!" Jesus then said, "Well then, pay to the Emperor what belongs to the Emperor and to whom you believe

in what belong to him."[47] That is the end of the story of truth. In my view, what belong to whom?

Take a quarter out of your pocket. Is that a face of an emperor or a king? And whose name is on all our coins, and the statement "In God We Trust"? Not trust in man or government! President Andrew Johnson put the name of God on coins for the first time in 1865, on the first printing of a real coin after the Civil War.[48] Wikipedia states: "In God We Trust" first appeared on the two-cent piece in 1864, and has appeared on paper currency since 1957 by joint resolution by the 84th Congress (P.L.84-140) and approved by Dwight D Eisenhower on July 30, 1956.[49]

The face on the quarter is not an emperor or a king, but the father of our country, George Washington. There is a story about an Indian chief meeting face to face with George Washington. The Indian chief told him that if they fired at him; his horse would be killed, but he would not. Then the Indian chief said, "I have travelled a long way to meet you. You were a young warrior, of a great battle. I come to pay homage to the man who is the particular favorite of Heaven, and who can never be killed in battle."[50] That story of history was in our textbooks for nearly a century and a half. Today it is absent, just as the others. We've been in the rabbit hole for a very long time.

Genesis of the Electoral College

James Wilson founded the Electoral College. Some time ago on talk radio, there was a man called Neal Bortz. He explained the Electoral College in this way. Say you own stock in a company. Your stock represents your percentage of ownership of the company. You are a free holder of that company. You receive a letter from the company, stating they are going to have a stockholders meeting to elect a new C.E.O., since the present C.E.O. passed away. You attend the meeting. One woman and four men, one of whom is a black man, are being considered. They all give their qualifications and you take their papers to study at home. No one is allowed in the meeting except stockholders. The workers in the factory do not vote, but some workers who own stock are authorized to vote. At the next meeting, everyone is handed a small paper and a pen to vote. The stockholders hand in their paper, with their choice on it, to the head desk where they are counted, and there is a tie between the woman and the black man. Another vote is taken and the person with the most votes becomes the new C.E.O. simple, but efficient.

After reading how a company and the Electoral College work to elect CEO and the chief magistrate of the country. The stockholders were the electors unless you read how simple and foolproof it is to protect the country. Why change it?

Would you not protect your land or investment from losing your stock or your liberty or the republic?

In the election of 1824 just as in today's Congress, we have different groups of organizations like caucus. Like the D.S.A. Party working with the congressional progressive caucus and other caucuses?[94]

Looking backward and then forward again to today's technology or today's technocracy. In my view, the jigsaw puzzle box without a picture is starting to make sense, before the last piece is in place, for that is an AHHA moment. Everything that I have researched is there for you to think about the book, Henry Clay, the 14th chapter is the most important. By Robert V. Reminius From the U.S. Archives.

They were trying to change this Republic to a Democracy in 1824 and what do the people think today? It's a Democracy and we have the popular vote and look who is crying now, the educated. We've had the Democratic vote for the President for the last 196 years. But who or what controlled the college for the 196 years? Usually in the beginning of the Republic. The Secretary of State became the President. From Jefferson to J.Q. Adams, then Clay didn't make it. Then Buchanan did, but after that, the VP would become President or someone slipped in somehow, like Lincoln and Kennedy and Trump? 2020 is the BIG ONE and all they have to do is get rid of Trump.

Below James Butler Anti-Fed Papers on Page 166 how simply it works to protect the Union from cabal, corruption, and conspiracy which are in effect today. For those who read the manual.

Mr. James Butler Anti-Papers Page 166:

Makes electoral College clear, to protect the Union "As the electors would vote at the same time throughout the United States at so great a distance from each other. The great evil of a cabal was avoided. It would be impossible to corrupt them from foreign influence."

Other remarks were similar form Madison, Pinckney, Gov. Morris page 159.

The unconstitutional nominations of the candidates for presidency and vice-presidency of the United States. The 1824 caucus wanted a popular vote.

1 – "A caucus nomination is against the spirit of the Constitution.

2 – It is expedient and impolitic.

3 – Members of Congress may become the final electors and therefore ought not prejudge the case by pledging themselves previously to support particular candidates.

4 – It violates the equality intended to be secured by the Constitution to the weaker states.

5 – Caucus nominations may in time acquire the force of precedents and become authoritative and thereby endanger the liberties of the people."[92]

The Declaration of Jefferson Removed from Declaration with Others

"He has waged cruel war against human nature itself, violating its most sacred right of life and liberty in the person of distant people who never offended him. Captivating and carrying them into slavery in another hemisphere or to incur miserable death in their transportation thither. This piratical warfare the opprobrium of infidel powers is the warfare of the Christian King of Great Britain. Determined to keep open a market where men should be sold and bought. He was prostituted his negative for suppressing every legislative attempt to prohibit or to restrain this execrable commerce and that this assemblage of horrors might want to fact distinguished die. He is now exciting those very people to rise in arms among us and to them. By murdering the people whom he also obtruded them thus paying of former crimes committed against the liberties of one people with the crimes of another."

Reading this above is Jefferson telling the King of Great Britain, you brought these horrors to this land and we are your subject under your royal commands. 157 years of blacks in British rule 1619 – 1776 it was slave labor before 1787 I think all our ancestors were slaves, brown yellow red black and white.

I Recall the quote by Thomas Jefferson saying, "What farmer, what laborer, or what mechanic will ever see a tax collector of the United States?"56 President Lincoln did not tax the poor, but the wealthiest section of society, when he imposed an income tax for the first time in the history of our union.85 As we learn more about the founding of our nation we discover what kind of men set up this Constitutional Representative Republic for you and I. It was as a great experiment in governing ourselves, with just laws, a Bill of Rights, and the abolishment of slavery. Until our founding fathers wrote our Constitution that broke the yoke that freed the world, we were all slaves.

Think about this for a moment. There is no pre-established body making the choice for you, like the Jackass and Elephant parties; no desire of a foreign power involved. The only thing that Neal Bortz didn't answer was who chose the candidates in the first place? It does not work this way. But at least there isn't any money involved, no ABC, CBS, NBC, CNN, PBS, or FOX (the media). That's a plus. The last election was $1 Billion, that was yours and my money.

Just stop for a moment; can you name five people, one of whom you would put on a paper to hand to the District of Columbia? Not too many left is there? The popular vote started in 1824. There is no statute, proven on record, for a popular vote! Yet, here is how it broke down.[51]

1824 Vote	Elector Votes	Popular Votes
John Q. Adams Democratic-Republican Party	84	108,740
Andrew Jackson Democratic-Republican Party	99	153,544

Who won? Do you know the answer? What happened? Read the history books. *Henry Clay, Statesman of the Union* – start with the 14th chapter. Alexander Hamilton wrote of The Electoral College in *Publius #68*:

If the method is not perfect, it is at least excellent. No Senator or Representative, or other persons holding a place of trust or profit under the United States, can be an elector. Nor, would I behest to suddenly start a corrupt conspiracy. To achieve this objective, the men who make the decision will be chosen by the people, at the appropriate time. For a specific purpose, rather than having any pre-established bodies make that decision. Every practical obstacle against a cabal, intrigue and corruption must be erected. These most deadly adversaries must be approached and expected from more than one quarter, but chiefly from the desire of foreign powers to gain improper influence in our council. How better to do this, than raising a creature of their own to the Chief Magistrate of the Union.[52]

In the archival history of many universities of that time, from *The Anti-Federalist Papers*, notes that James Wilson discovered that the Republic of Poland protected itself with an electoral college.[53] Wilson provided this information to the Constitutional Congress. The Poland Story showed how a country protected itself from a collectivist cabal, corruption, and foreign influence. Governor Morris created the requirement that electors be freeholders, in other words, they must own property. The idea was that you had something of value so you would feel a sense of responsibility, trust; that you owned part of the country. Most men owned property, and their wives inherited the land upon their passing. Free black men, who started as indentured servants and now owned property, bought land and hired other black men as indentured servants. So right from the beginning, any man, woman, or black man could have been an elector. At that time, voting rights pertained to men alone, the world was very different then.

James Wilson, of *The Anti-Federalist Papers*, stated: "I am bold to assert that this Constitution is the best form of government which has ever been offered to the world". [54]

I learned of the idea that, "In religion, the preacher is apt to forget the Creator", first proposed on the floor of the convention in Philadelphia in 1787 by Governor Morris, *Anti-Federalist Papers* pgs. 107-109.

The "rich" will strive to establish their dominion and enslave the rest; they always have and always will. The proper security against this is to form them into a separate interest allowing the two forces to then control each other. Let the rich mix with the poorer and in a commercial enterprise, they will establish an "oligarchy". Take the commerce away, and a democracy will triumph. Thus it has been the entire world over; so it will be among us also. Reason tells us we are but men and we are not to expect any particular interference of Heaven in our favor. Being combined against this danger, there will be a mutual check and mutual security. A firm government alone can protect our liberties but fears the influences of the rich. The rich will have the same effect here, as elsewhere, if we do not, by such a government, keep them within their proper sphere. The rich will take advantage of their passion and make these the instruments for oppression. The result of the contest will be a violent aristocracy or a more violent despotism.[55]

Reading the above, what ran through your mind? The founders of this Republic wanted a homogenous aristocracy with the most numerous of the new society to work together harmoniously. They did not want the rich to oppress the society workers but pay them a living wage; enough to pay for their retirement and affordable healthcare under a free enterprise, inflation proof system, with gold or silver coinage. In other words, exactly what our Founders proposed in 1787. Read the instruction manual. Ask yourself, would you rather have a $20 paper dollar or a $20 gold coin in your vault?

DONT TREAD ON ME

What May Be Forbidden

Hamilton #30 could never imagine a 25-cent chip in 1787.

My main interest in the address, in *The Anti-Federalist Papers* by Samuel Bryan, is in our Constitution; Article One, Section Nine which states:

"No capitation or other direct tax shall be laid, unless in proportion to the census, or enumeration herein before directed to be taken."

The Anti-Federalist Papers are where to find where this section, under the title of Centinel. It's a must read on the subject of the people of this time. The piece first appeared at the convention on December 12, by Samuel Bryan, though the article was not signed.

"We have before considered internal taxation, as it would affect the destruction of the State government and produce one consolidated government. We will now consider that subject, as it affects the personal concerns of the people. The power of direct taxation applies to every individual, as Congress under this government is expressly vested with the authority of laying a capitation, or poll tax, upon every person to any amount. This is a tax that, however oppressive in its nature and unequal in its operation is certain, as to produce and simple in its collection; it cannot be evaded like the object of imports or excise, and will be paid, because all that a man hath will he give for his head. <u>This is so congenial to the nature of despotism, that it has ever been a favorite under such government.</u> Some of those who were in the late general convention from the State have long labored to introduce a poll tax among us." [57]

"The power of direct taxation will further apply to every individual, as Congress may tax land, cattle, <u>trades</u>, occupations, etc. in any amount, and every object of internal taxation is of that nature, however oppressive. The people will have but the alternative to pay the tax, or let their property be taken. For all resistance to pay will be in vain. The standing army and select militia would enforce the collection. There is not even a declaration of rights which the people may appeal for the vindication of their wrongs in the covets of justice. They must therefore implicitly obey the most arbitrary laws. The conduct of administration, responsibility of the people will not exist in this government. The members of the legislature are taken from among the people, and their interest and welfare are so inseparably connected to their constituents that they can serve no advantage from oppressive laws and taxes, for they would suffer in common with their fellow citizens; would participate in the burdens they impose on the community, as they must return to the common level after a short period, and not withstanding every exertion of influence; every means of corruption. A necessary rotation excludes them from permanency in the legislature." [58]

Publius #30 to #36 is a must read! It discusses the power needed for taxation: It is the most important read in my thesis together.

Publius #30 by Hamilton:

"What substitute can be imagined for this **angus fatuus** in finance, but that of permitting the federal government to raise its own revenue by ordinary methods of taxation, authorized in every well-ordered constitution of civil government? Ingenious men my proclaim with plausibility on any subject, but no human ingenuity can point out any other expedient to rescue us.'[59] $26 trillion debt.

Can a 25-cent poker chip change our world?

Revisiting *Publius #36* by Alexander Hamilton, we learn:

As to the suggestion of double taxation, the answer is plain. The wants of the union are to be supplied in one way or another; if to be done by the authority of the Federal government, it will not be done by that of the State governments. The quantity of taxes to be paid by the community must be the same in either case with the advantage if the provision is to be made by the Union. That the capital resources of commercial imports, which is the most convenient branch of revenue, can be prudently improved to a much greater extent under Federal than under State regulations, and of course will render it less necessary to recur to more inconvenient methods; and with this further advantage, that as far as there may be any real difficulty in the exercise of the power of internal taxation, it will impose a disposition to greater care in the choice and arrangement of the means, <u>and must naturally tend to make a fixed point of policy in the National Administration to go as far as may be practicable in making the luxury of the rich tributary to the public treasury</u>, in order to diminish the necessity of those impositions which might create dissatisfaction on the poorer and most numerous classes of the society. Happy it is when the interest which the government has in its preservation of its own power, coincides with the proper distribution of the public burdens and tend to guard the least wealthy part of the community from oppression.[59]

Here it is important to understanding the meanings of certain words used in the *Publius*, quoted above.

Tributary (n): [60]

> a. A stream or river that flows into a larger one
>
> b. Paying tribute, making additions or furnishing supplies; contribution

Tribute (n): [61]

> a. A payment by one ruler or nation to another in acknowledgment of submission or as the price of protection also the tax levied for such a payment
>
> b. An excessive tax, rental, or tariff imposed by a government, sovereign, lord, or landlord
>
> c. An exorbitant charge levied by a person or group having the power of coercion
>
> d. The liability to pay tribute

Burden (n): [62]

a. Anything carried or endured (passed on)

b. A very heavy load, hard to bear (debt)

c. A load weigh down, oppressive (Federal Reserve)

DONT TREAD ON ME

The Roman Empire

The importance of introducing Jamual Bryan into this perspective is the burden that the two parties have put the middle class, and most numerous of the society with a burden of over twenty-two plus trillion-dollar debt. That we must borrow to keep the economy alive plus an internal tax or poll tax on you and me?

Now the parties are thinking about a fair tax to pay to get rid of the debt. Look it up. Its HR. 25 date 1-7-2003 by John Lender, of GA. A fair tax of 23% [92] on everything you buy, including food. Must we be deceived again to be happy. Remember Dostoyevski? A baby born in 2016 accepts a debt of $42,537.88 for each of us also. And it's higher now and that is also yours and mine.

Now let's go back to the Roman Empire in 55 BC, there was a giant in the Roman Senate called Marcus Tullius Cicero[66], born January 6, 106 BC and died at 63, 43 BC.

Cicero was not a born again Christian but had virtue far beyond the times. I will quote what he said form my cliff notes:

"Do not blame Caesar, blame the people for wanting more money, more ease, more security, more living fatally at the expense of the industrious."

And on the floor of the Roman Senate:

"The budget should be balanced.

The treasury should be rebuilt

The public debit should be reduced

The officialdom should be tempered, and foreign land be curtailed. Less Rome becomes bankrupt. People must learn to work instead of living on public assistance."

After the fall of the Roman Empire, the citizens of Rome were waiting for the barbarians to come. Foreign aliens, primitive savages to come into Rome and sack the city. It might have been the answer. They would have to fight for Rome. Is this the picture of our republic in 2020 election is only months away?

It's A Republic If We Are Allowed to Keep It

The first seven centuries of Rome were filled with military power. Technology was changing weapons. Copper to iron swords, cross bows etc. the color of red stained the ground, east and west and again to the Holy land. Popes and emperors governed the same.

This constitutional republic is only 232 years old. Rome lasted about 1500 years, with tyrants, popes, emperors, aristocrats and slaves. That was the world before 1787. Oppression of the most numerous of the societies.

The United States fought two world wars, rebuilt Europe with our money, marshal plan. Bailout social democracies all with our internal tax that was to be a temporary tax for emergencies. Jefferson[56] and Lincoln[85] understood what you are about to read seriously in their speeches and deeds. *Publius#36*

Talk radio is very important to me. Two gentlemen interviewed on two opposite stations. Both were about the same subject. Webster Tarpley, a historian on economic and the other was Mr. Charles Collins a candidate for the magistrate in 1995. Both said the same thing. On Wall Street, there are over a quadrillion transaction a year and if we could charge a percentage of that world casino we could pay our debit.

I am not much of a gambler. When in California, my buddies and I went to Gardenia, CA to play poker at their casino. I won a pot of chips. The crupia took a 25ct chip out of my winnings and put it into the slot on the table. I asked what are you doing? The crupia said that's for the house. I looked around, everything was new and shiny and cool and all of us had a free drink. Okay. I didn't win again.

As I read the federalists' papers 30-36 about direct, poll tax, internal and income tax and Samuel Bryans description about it being so congenial to the nature of despotism, that it has been a favorite under such a government. But this republic has been so weakened, that this next election, 2020 could be critical.

But you are going to read *Publius#36* and if you are able to understand it like I am. Let's go to work right now! The Federalist Papers are the most authoritative commentary on the United States Constitution. It has a quality of legitimacy, authority and authenticity. In the meaning, genuine meaning of "men acting by virtue of powers, may not only what their powers do not authorize, but what they forbid." What was always referred to at the impeachment of _Donaldo Trumptius_ *Maximus*. If you agree with #36, the answer by our founders is clear. That when the debit gets so voluminous, that no man or woman knows what it is today and can only guess what it will be in the future. Will it be bankruptcy or back to normality. I'm not pretending to be an expert on the papers. I only use my left brain or right brain. If my thinking is correct "section 7, Article one, all bills for raising revenue shall originate in the House of Representatives shall become law and the President is presented with it." It states in #36, happy it is when the interests of the government has in its preservation of its own power. Coincides with the proper distribution of public burdens and of guarding the least wealthy part of the community from oppression.[59] In order to save the peoples' republic, one more judicial appointment by *Trumptius Maximus* would get the tenor of our constitution on its ground floor again.

DONT TREAD ON ME

Something Imagined, a Poker Chip

In thinking about taxing Wall Street with a percentage tax you can't tax each stock but you could tax each transaction, so when I remember winning a pot in a casino and they took a chip of 25ct for the house, I said to myself, why can't we use a excise tax of 50ct times a trillion. This seems to be a small amount to pay for our debt. So that is where that thought came from and when I told others they said, yes, so let's do it now.

a. Anything carried or endured (passed on)

b. A very heavy load, hard to bear (debt)

c. A load weigh down, oppressive (Federal Reserve)

Remember what Governor Morris wrote in *The Anti-Federalist Papers*. Go back and read what he said, "The rich will strive to establish their dominion and enslave the rest."[64] That was the old world order of kings, one-man rule, and banks. This Republic stopped that, and they want it back, with the new kings and their wealthy banks, to dominate and enslave. Donald Trump, "Donaldo Maximus", dealt with the moneyed entities in Manhattan, N.Y. and needed to save this Republic. He's a romantic, as we are, who believes in this Constitutional Republic. After reading *Publius #30 and #36* by Alexander Hamilton, did you ever expect to discover that the men in the convention would plan, for some time in our future, when the moneyed entities appear with a new world approach? Or that if we don't support the President it may be over?

Remember that the population of our nation is larger than the media would have us believe at 328.7 million. The invasion of immigrants from Central America through Mexico over the last several years is not in our favor. My firm belief is that we need to stop all immigration until we get our house in order, and then have specific rules and requirements for whom we let in. If we review again the law during the L.B.J. S500 Administration, in 1965, that affected immigration policy, we see that even 53 years ago we were allowing 900,000 immigrants into our country along with their families per year. Do the math! That's 47 million immigrants over the last 53 years – not including their families!

If we look at some of the disparity between the rich and the poor in this country, we see that the wealthy are increasing exponentially and there is no reason for it to change. We cannot do without them.

Wealth Distribution Among U.S. Population[65]
1% of the population, 32.7 million people, own 35% of the wealth in the US.
4% of the population, 88.6 million people, own 27% of the wealth in the US.
5% of the population, 36 million people, own 11% of the wealth in the US.
10% of the population, 39 million people, own 12% of the wealth in the US.
The Upper Middle Class, 20% of the population, 36 million people, own 11% of the wealth in the US.
The Middle Class, 20% of the population, 36 million people, own 4% of the wealth in the US.
The bottom 40% of the population, 131 million people, own <1% of the wealth in the US.

Disclaimer: This is an official document from the United States government which is not very clear and does not align with my thinking and my readings.

The 32.7 million people, 1% of the population, control 35% of the wealth generated by industry, corporations, land, factories, railroads, production and distribution, banks and capitalists, Trillionaires, Billionaires, Millionaires, most of whom invest on Wall Street. Some or most have tax-free foundations that support Democratic or Republican ideas and the liberal media with foundation money.

The next 88.6 million people own 4% of the wealth. These people own small businesses, stores, service providers, auto agencies, and franchises.

The largest faction of the U.S. population, 40% or 131 million, you and me, own <1% of the wealth of the U.S. We worked in the factories and in the corporations, and industries that are owned by those who own 35% of the country's wealth. By moving their factories and our jobs overseas, these "owners" removed approximately $14 trillion dollars from our country, greatly diminishing the opportunities for those of us at the bottom of the wealth funnel, working as laborers in various industries. By doing this, leaving so many of us without jobs, tax revenue decreased. The non-wealthy classes are essentially no longer able to pay the taxes to fund the schools where the illegal immigrants are educating their children. No longer can we fund the entitlements being given to 131 million people living below the poverty line in America. We can only hope that current and future leaders create factory jobs so that the working middle class can again see full employment.

Marcus Tullious Cicero, a Roman Senator, stated on the floor of the Senate:

> A nation can survive its fools and its ambitions, but it cannot survive treason from within. An enemy, at its gates is less formidable, for he carries his banner openly against the city. A traitor within rots out the soul of a nation.[66]

Thomas Jefferson, the third president, who was also a read-head like Trump, said, "The interest and loyalties of capitalists, transcends national territories, merchants and capitalists, have no country of their own. They have no soul or soil of their own.[67]

They moved our jobs overseas – isn't that treason? We can't wait twenty years to rebuild our treasury on the back of the 200 million middle class workers by burdening them with a "fair" tax of 23% on every purchase made overseas, as was decreed under Presidents Nixon, Ford, Carter, Reagan, Bush I, Clinton, Bush II. President Obama then changed part-time jobs to 30 hours a week. Now workers have no medical and no retirement, the start of socialism.

We've been in Afghanistan for ten years, yet they did not attack us. And if we are not going to build a pipeline from the Caspian Sea, to Pakistan, to the Indian Ocean, then what are we doing there? You can't democratize Islam. To show you how deep in the rabbit hole we now are, we now have an Islamist representative, from Wisconsin, what does she know about a republic? She knows nothing and so does this country. No! Enough nonsense.

According to the United States Deposit Trust Clearing Corporation, there are huge transactions on the New York Stock Exchange. In a given year there are over a trillion transactions, that's one followed by fifteen zeros. Wall Street trades, stock options, futures, hedge funds, flash trades, on a bank of computers, derivatives and others – it's the big world casino.

The British have used a Financial Transaction Tax (F.T.T) on their stock exchange for many of years at a cost of only .05% of their revenue and derived four billion pounds a year doing so. Japan has also used the F.T.T., drawing 4.0% of their federal tax to their treasury in 1980.

The United States also had a small F.T.T. from 1914 to 1980 and of course, we did away with it. So the F.T.T. is not new, and it can put a lot of money into our non-existent treasury in one year.

Hypothetically speaking, it works this way: say you buy $30,000.00 of General Electric Stock (GE). Your write a check for $30,000.00 plus your broker's fee. But, now you add an F.T.T., an excise tax of $0.50, when you buy and sell. The Financial Transaction Tax (F.T.T.) the buyer needs to pay based on Article 1, Section 8, of the U.S. Constitution says that an excise tax of $0.50 must be paid on every trade, buy or sell.

Think about this. The first year after they imagined the future that Hamilton could not substitute for the federal government. A 25-cent chip at a gambling table may be the solution for the federal gov. the state gov. the same as the federal gov. imagine something? But it's the two party system. The bill is passed with the utmost Constitutional standards we would have tribute in our treasury, of what amount, maybe enough to pay our debts and maybe more? I don't know how far we could go with this. But, the new bill must have provisions in it to start over with our Constitutional Representative Republic again. If we do not return to the tenor of our Republic as written by the people three hundred and thirty-two years ago there would be no point, if we don't go back to our roots to have a F.T.T. nothing will change.

If the F.T.T. were to be granted, we could lower it to what is needed annually, to $0.05 or $0.10 or $0.15, for our national budget and we could do away with the oppressive Poll Tax. Isn't this better than accepting socialism and the oppression that goes with it? In 1789 Benjamin Franklin said, "It's a Republic if you can keep it."[65]

Today, it's a republic if we the people are allowed to keep it.

These are my opinions of reading the "instruction manual".

Love and gratitude to those men, who with their wisdom made a system of government for all to live free and independent as long as we read the "instruction books".

Our founders knew the rich would start to oppress us again with unwinnable wars, move our factories and jobs, and elect socialist democracies. This brings them up and brings us down so as to create equality. We understand factions, because we read about them and their effects on societies, good societies, and their danger to our Constitutional Republic. And this book, *The Federalist Papers,* is so important to our curriculum. We, as a society, have no idea what happened to the two-party system. If we had read *Publius #68* in *The Federalist Papers* it is stated that the founding fathers did not trust parties to make the decision to elect the Chief Magistrate of our country. And if you're honest with yourself, look at the amount of money, almost a billion dollars, spent just on this last election. Where does this money come from? I call the Republicans the Elephants and the Democrats the Jackasses. Where does the big money come from? Remember Governor Morris said, "The rich will strive to establish their dominion and enslave the rest. They always do and they always will." [66]

They Want It Back

The new world order crowd was all set to take over with Hillary Clinton, but the Electoral College, which is to protect the smaller states from this cancer, did its job. But in the 21st Century, it's the cities that are the danger to the Republic with their entitlements, illegal, socialist Jackass Mayors and Governors. This is what Madison's *Publius #10* was talking about, factions. And the Jackass crowd wants Democracy. Recall the quote, "they are always of contention and turbulence and their lives are is short as their deaths are violent and they hate others for their discontent."[70]

Publius #10 states, "Factions are the moral disease, by which popular Governments have perished everywhere".[71] This new world order crowd with their fancy words like "proletariat" and "bourgeoisie" are dictators which remind me of the story of the Bourg on Star Trek, The Next Generation. Everyone on the Bourg was politically equal and correct, thought the same, looked and felt the same, and they destroyed every civilization in the universe that didn't assimilate with them because "resistance was futile". The total answer is not yet clear. But the jigsaw puzzle picture is beginning to become clearer. When the last piece is in place that will be the "Ah Ha" moment. That's when everyone says, "look at what the wealth of the world tried to do to us workers of the world, especially, the Americans of North America with their Constitution". Let's keep this republic, stop this nonsense of socialism, and save this world from oppression. As it says in *The Anti-Federalist* papers and *The Federalist Papers* the old system of kings, emperors, one family rule is over.

Karl Marx coined the words "capitalism". The word does not appear in *The Federalist Papers* or *The Anti-Federalist Papers*. Thomas Jefferson is the only one who used the word "capitalist" in one of his writings. It's always been laissez-faire, without government regulation or control. What made America great? It was a fair wage, quality, and abundance. The working class of America, earning a fair wage, built a middle-class society under free enterprise. When did America change?

My view is that it started with McKinley's Spanish American War. Our jurisdiction went from longitude 60° West to longitude 120° East. We became imperialists, from the coast of Maine to the Philippine Islands.

These are my opinions, based on my studies of these Papers and world events from 1950 to today regarding the new world order that is evolving. I read about people involved with this "new world order crowd", from 1950 forward. Arthur M. Schlesinger Jr., author, historian, and CFR member stated, "We are not going to achieve a new world order without paying for it in blood as well as in words and money." [72] David Rockefeller, addressing the media in 1960 stated, "But the world is more sophisticated and prepared to march toward a world government."[73] Thus we see both sides of the argument as it emerges. We are on the verge of a global transformation; all we need is the right major crisis and the nation will accept a new world order such as The Council of Foreign Relations (CFR).

The 1990 Monetary Act, created by the International Monetary Fund (IMF), invented a system by which bank to bank transfers of wealth from the rich nation to the poor nations could take place. Before this, in 1971, a group I call OPIC "The Overseas Private Investment Corp"[86] made up of Nixon, Kissinger, and Rockefeller, went to china, a third world, and arranged to move our industry and manufacturing there after joining the United Nations arranged to move our industry and manufacturing there after joining the United Nations. And voila, you have the World Trade Organization (WTO).

It's A Republic If We Are Allowed to Keep It

In Foreign Affairs Magazine in 1974, it was written that our leaders would, "Slowly pull over the eyes of the American people moving our factories overseas."[74] In his 1976 book, Henry Kissinger wrote, "The time of the U.S. is over. We must negotiate for a position. First to use the new world order."[75] In his 1970 book *Between two Ages*, by Zbigniew Brzezinski writes, "Deliberate management of the American future with planners as a key for legislators and manipulators"[76] On February 17, 1950, James Paul Warburg confidently declared to the United States Senate: "We shall have World Government, whether or not we like it. The only question is whether World Government will be achieved by conquest or consent.[77] Warburg and Aldrich had something to do about, the Federal Reserve becoming law.

In the 1960s David Rockefeller, in a statement to the public said:

> We are grateful to the New York Times, Newsweek, the Washington Times, and other great publications whose directors have attended our meetings and respected these policies of discretion for all these 40 years. It would have been impossible for the U.S. to develop our plan for the world if we had been subject to the bright lights of publicity during these years. But the world is more sophisticated and prepared to march toward a world government. The super national sovereignty of interlocking elite and world bankers is surely preferable to the national

determination practiced in the last centuries. [78]

The majority of the nations of this world have voted in social democratic governments in Spain, England, France, Austria, Greece, Italy, Scotland and Ireland, predominantly in first world countries. The other nations are governed by tyrants, dictators, one-man rule, or ruled by Islam. I can't name them all but you get the sense of it.

The first world countries have voted in some of the liberal ideas. The citizens can vote to create entitlements, universal medical coverage, and other things, by certain measures or propositions created by a faction. These factions are passionate, loud and hate the other for their discomfort although they have common interest and passion for our country. In a democracy, the majority of the whole will almost always feel suffering. There is nothing to keep the force in check, so the weakest part of the society doesn't suffer from obnoxious individuals who usually create another "ism".

In 1787 the founders of The Constitutional Representative Republic knew that people could vote in anything they wanted and would destroy the Republic and that any statute that was presented on the floor of the House would be null and void. In Star Trek the Bourg was a cube going through the universe destroying every planet that did not assimilate with them, for "resistance is futile". This is an apropos metaphor for how a faction is defined in *Publius #10* of the *Federalist Papers*. Madison wrote that, "Factions have destroyed every popular society in world history."[75]

Napoleon, Marx, and Lenin, men all in the age of revolution, as well as some in the nineteenth century, were planning for twenty-first century security and put forth a plan for a new world order. You can look it up for yourself and find the jigsaw puzzle box without a picture on it. When you put the puzzle together, you will then see exactly what I fear.

In a statement on the floor of The House of Commons in 1864, and reported in the London Times, Banking Edition the following statement was made:

> If that mischievous financial policy, which had its origin in the North American Republic during the late war, Civil War, should become indurated down to a fixture. Then that government will furnish its own money without cost. It will pay off its debt and be without debt. It will have all the money necessary to carry on its commerce. It will become prosperous beyond any president in history. The brains and wealth of all countries will go to North America. That government must be destroyed or it will destroy every monarchy on the globe.[79]

Max Warburg wrote, "President Lincoln printed greenbacks without paying the German bank twenty-three percent interest."[80]

In 1928 Adolf Hitler said, "National Socialism will be the avenue to a new word order". [81] Dostoyevsky wrote, "You must be deceived to be happy".

[82] And, I often say, "so soon old, so late smart."

So, what have we gained from this reading? Two books? No! Three books - *The Federalist Papers*, *The Anti-Federalist Papers*, and *The Bible*. These books are the foundation of our country. In the farewell address of our first president, George Washington, he covered many of these warnings, but I like this one the best:

> Happiness never can be expected of a nation that disregards the eternal rules of order and right, which heaven itself has ordained and since the preservation of the sacred fire of liberty and the destiny of the republic model of government, are justly considered on the experiment entrusted to the hands of the American people.[83]

In this new century, the "moneyed creatures" are apt to forget all the good books that were to keep us cognizant of the laws of justice. Secularism has destroyed our faith in justice, free enterprise, not capitalism, coined by Marx. The only place I can find the word capitalism by our founders is when Thomas Jefferson writes, "The interest and loyalties if capitalism transcends national territories. Where they may be they have no ties with the soil". [84] The real world example in our time is the moving of our industries to China. Remember what Governor Morris said – go find it and read it again. Capitalism means money, the wealthy. As Governor Morris continues he shows that there should be an oligarchy with the poor and the rich.

However, we have lost that cognizance of faith because we do not have these three books in the classrooms in our schools. This new government, a republic based on morality and faith in the rule of law, can stand up against this abomination of dishonesty, insincerity, disloyalty, and breaking of the promise of faith. Our Jackass and Elephant leaders have dishonesty told us that we are a democracy, but our faith in them is gone.

Now, to bring all this to a close, not with a lot of feeling, but with a thoughtful conclusion. Today we have the Jackass Party accusing the Elephant Party of being Nazi's, like Hitler. However, the record shows, as do my many years of "cliff notes" that as Adolf Hitler said in 1928, "National Socialism will be the avenue to a new world order."

On the other side, the Elephant Party is listening to the candidates of the Jackass Party running for the Chief Magistrate of our country wanting to change this Nation, which is a Constitutional Representative Republic, into a democracy. We were given *The Federalist and Anti-Federalist Papers* as the "instruction manual" for running our country well. Sadly, these important *Papers* are not taught at any level of our educational system, with the possible exception of Hillsdale College and a very few others.

Once a country accepts a democracy, it would be very easy to change the Constitutional Representative Republic into another "ism" by just one vote. For that one vote would then be a majority. Like Senator

McCain of Arizona did, with the Emperor of Rome vote, with the thumbs down vote on the floor of the Senate.

Now I know everyone knows this but, the Union of the Soviet Socialist Republics was a communist country. However, both my "cliff notes" and the dictionary state that Soviet Russia was a Union of Soviet Socialist Republics with a body of delegates, The Bureau of the Communist Party. This was the core of the leadership of the Soviet Union, much like we have with the Jackass and Elephant Parties, two parties, which are to represent the oath of their allegiance, being loyal, steadfast and devoted to the Constitutional Republic. They act as a representative of the people and their parties, which our founding fathers discouraged. They were to keep a promise, swear the truth, to swear solemnly. You cannot say it better than this. Every statute must support the Constitution or it weakens our Republic as it says in *Publius #78* of *The Federalist Papers* written by Alexander Hamilton. This loyalty has been broken many times. The most profound statement in *Publius #78* is this, "that men acting by virtue of powers may not do only what their powers do not authorize, but what they forbid…or, in other words, he Constitution ought to be preferred to the statute, the intention of the people to the intention of their agents". [81]

This was the intent of our original agents 232 years ago. The Soviet Union was only 107 years old, half the age of this Republic. Russia is also a republic; their intent is to socialize the world. Our intent was to be an example to the world. As Thomas Jefferson wrote to Elbridge Gerry, 26

January 1799:

> I am for a government rigorously frugal and simple, I am for
> commerce with all nations, political connections with none, and
> little or no diplomatic establishment. I am not linking us by new
> treaties with the quarrels of Europe, entering that field of slaughter,
> to preserve their balance or joining in the confederacy of king to
> war against the principles of liberty.[82]

The question is, do we stick to the tenor of our script or go back to
the dark ages of royalty? The rich have always oppressed the masses as
Governor Morris said; you read the warnings that are in *The Papers*.

The Soviet Union had the same oath. Men acting by virtue of
Soviet Power may not do only what their powers do not authorize, but
what they forbid. Did the Soviet Socialist represent well born, the wealthy,
or you?

Notes

[1] Ketcham, Ralph. *The Anti-Federalist Papers and the Constitutional Convention Debates.* (New York: Signet Classic, 1986), 110.

[2] Ketcham, Ralph. *The Anti-Federalist Papers and the Constitutional Convention Debates.* (New York: Signet Classic, 1986), 188.

[3] Ketcham, Ralph. *The Anti-Federalist Papers and the Constitutional Convention Debates.* (New York: Signet Classic, 1986), 107.

[4] "United States of America (USA) Population," Country Meters, accessed April 19, 2019, https://countrymeters.info/en/United_states_of_america_(USA).

[5] Tatiana Schlossberg, "The State of Publishing: Literacy Rates," McSweeney's Internet Tendency, February 7, 2011, accessed April 19, 2019, https://www.mcsweeneys.net/articles/literacy-rates.

[6] Rossiter, Clinton. *The Federalist Papers.* (New York: Signet Classic, 1961.), 467.

[7] Rossiter, Clinton. *The Federalist Papers.* (New York: Signet Classic, 1961.), 241.

[8] Ibid.

[9] Rossiter, Clinton. *The Federalist Papers.* (New York: Signet Classic, 1961.), 70-71.

[10] Rossiter, Clinton. *The Federalist Papers.* (New York: Signet Classic, 1961.), 413.

[11] *Miriam Webster Dictinoary, s.v.* "faction", accessed April 27, 2019, https://www.merriam-webster.com/dictionary/faction.

[12] Rossiter, Clinton. *The Federalist Papers.* (New York: Signet Classic, 1961.), 78.

[13] *U.S. Constitution - Article 4 Section 4.* accessed April 27, 2019, https://www.usconstitution.net/xconst_A4Sec4.html.

[14] Rossiter, Clinton. *The Federalist Papers.* (New York: Signet Classic, 1961.), 81.

It's A Republic If We Are Allowed to Keep It

[15] Ibid.

[16] Ketcham, Ralph. *The Anti-Federalist Papers and the Constitutional Convention Debates.* (New York: Signet Classic, 1986), 174-175.

[17] Rossiter, Clinton. *The Federalist Papers.* (New York: Signet Classic, 1961.), 395.

[18] Patrick Lee. "Thomas Jefferson on Plato's 'Philosophy'". Jefferson Leadership.com, September 23, 2011, accessed April 27, 2019, http://thomasjeffersonleadership.com/blog/thomas-jefferson-on-plato's-"philosophy"/#.

[19] Rossiter, Clinton. *The Federalist Papers.* (New York: Signet Classic, 1961.), 467.

[20] Ibid.

[21] Rossiter, Clinton. *The Federalist Papers.* (New York: Signet Classic, 1961.), 465.

[22] Rossiter, Clinton. *The Federalist Papers.* (New York: Signet Classic, 1961.), 465-466.

[24] Paul Leicester Ford. "The Works of Thomas Jefferson, 12 vols." Liberty Fund.org, accessed April 27, 2019, https://oll.libertyfund.org/titles/jefferson-the-works-vol-5-correspondence-1786-1789#Jefferson_0054-05_433

[25] Rossiter, Clinton. *The Federalist Papers.* (New York: Signet Classic, 1961.), 322.

[26] Garnett, Constance, translator. *The Brothers Karamazov.* By Fyodor Dostoyevsky. eBooks.Adelade.edu.au, December 27, 2014, accessed on April 28, 2019, https://ebooks.adelaide.edu.au/d/dostoyevsky/d72b/complete.html

[27] Rossiter, Clinton. *The Federalist Papers.* (New York: Signet Classic, 1961.), 322.

[28] Garnett, Constance, translator. *The Brothers Karamazov.* By Fyodor Dostoyevsky. eBooks.Adelade.edu.au, December 27, 2014, accessed on April 28, 2019, https://ebooks.adelaide.edu.au/d/dostoyevsky/d72b/complete.html

[29] Rossiter, Clinton. *The Federalist Papers.* (New York: Signet Classic, 1961.), 77.

[30] Rossiter, Clinton. *The Federalist Papers.* (New York: Signet Classic, 1961.), 313.

[31] Ketcham, Ralph. *The Anti-Federalist Papers and the Constitutional Convention Debates.* (New York: Signet Classic, 1986), 277.

[32] Ibid.

[33] *"Census 2000 Shows Resident Population of 281,421,906; Apportionment Counts Delivered to President".* United States Census Bureau.gov, accessed April 27, 2019, https://www.census.gov/newsroom/releases/archives/census_2000/cb00-cn64.html.

[34] "Public Law 89-236 To amend the Immigration and Nationality Act, and for other purposes." Govinfo.gov, accessed April 27, 2019, https://www.govinfo.gov/content/pkg/STATUTE-79/pdf/STATUTE-79-Pg911.pdf.

[35] Ibid.

[36] Bracero History Archive is a project of the Roy Rosenweig Center for History and New Media, George Mason University, the Smithsonian National Museum of American History, Brown University, and the Institute of Oral History at the University of Texas at El Paso. Funding provided by the National Endowment for the Arts, Bracero Archive.org, accessed April 30, 2019, http://braceroarchive.org/about.

[37] Rossiter, Clinton. *The Federalist Papers.* (New York: Signet Classic, 1961.), 467.

[38] Ibid.

[39] Rossiter, Clinton. *The Federalist Papers.* (New York: Signet Classic, 1961.), 301.

[40] "Luke 22:19, New Living Translation." BibleHub.com, accessed April 30, 2019, https://biblehub.com/luke/22-19.htm.

[41] "John 14:30-31, King James Version". BibleHub.com, accessed April 30, 2019, https://biblehub.com/kjv/john/14-30.htm

[42] Rossiter, Clinton. *The Federalist Papers.* (New York: Signet Classic, 1961.), 298.

[43] "The President and The Press: Address Before the American Newspaper Publishers Association, April 27, 1961." JFK Library.org, accessed April 30, 2019, https://www.jfklibrary.org/archives/other-resources/john-f-kennedy-speeches/american-newspaper-publishers-association-19610427.

[44] Rossiter, Clinton. *The Federalist Papers*. (New York: Signet Classic, 1961.), 370-371.

[45] Ketcham, Ralph. *The Anti-Federalist Papers and the Constitutional Convention Debates*. (New York: Signet Classic, 1986), 107.

[46] Rossiter, Clinton. *The Federalist Papers*. (New York: Signet Classic, 1961.), 81.

[47]"Mark12:17, GOD'S WORD®Translation." BibleHub.com, accessed April 30, 2019, https://biblehub.com/mark/12-17.htm.

[48] "In God We Trust", Wikipedia.com, accessed April 30, 2019, https://en.wikipedia.org/wiki/In_God_We_Trust .

[49] Ibid.

[50] "George Washington, Indian Chief TESTIFIES – 'He-Couldn't Die!", MinistersBest Friend.com, accessed April30, 2019, http://www.ministers-best-friend.com/George-Washington-Indian-Chief-TESTIFIES-He-Couldnt-be-killed.html.

[51] Major Dan, "History: December 1, 1824: Jackson Wins Popular Vote and Electoral Vote. Loses Election!", December 1, 2015, Accessed April 30, 2029, https://www.historyandheadlines.com/history-december-1-1824-jackson-wins-popular-vote-and-electoral-vote-loses-election/.

[52] Rossiter, Clinton. *The Federalist Papers*. (New York: Signet Classic, 1961.), 412-413.

[53] Ketcham, Ralph. *The Anti-Federalist Papers and the Constitutional Convention Debates*. (New York: Signet Classic, 1986), 115-116.

[54] Ketcham, Ralph. *The Anti-Federalist Papers and the Constitutional Convention Debates*. (New York: Signet Classic, 1986), 188.

[55] Ketcham, Ralph. *The Anti-Federalist Papers and the Constitutional Convention Debates*. (New York: Signet Classic, 1986), 107.

[56] Rossiter, Clinton. *The Federalist Papers*. (New York: Signet Classic, 1961.), 310-311.

[57] Ketcham, Ralph. *The Anti-Federalist Papers and the Constitutional Convention Debates*. (New York: Signet Classic, 1986), 252.

[58] "Wealth Inequality in the United States," Wikipedia, accessed April 22, 2019, https://en.wikipedia.org/wiki/Wealth_inequality_in_the_United_States.

[59] Rossiter, Clinton. *The Federalist Papers*. (New York: Signet Classic, 1961.), 142-143.

[60] Rossiter, Clinton. *The Federalist Papers*. (New York: Signet Classic, 1961.), 222.

[61] *Miriam Webster Dictinoary, s.v.* "tributary", accessed April 22, 2019, https://www.merriam-webster.com/dictionary/tributary.

[62] *Miriam Webster Dictinoary, s.v.* "tribute", accessed April 22, 2019, https://www.merriam-webster.com/dictionary/tribute.

[63]

Miriam Webster Dictinoary, s.v. "burden", accessed April 22, 2019, https://www.merriam-webster.com/dictionary/burden.

[64] Ketcham, Ralph. *The Anti-Federalist Papers and the Constitutional Convention Debates*. (New York: Signet Classic, 1986), 107.

[65] "United States of America (USA) Population," Country Meters, accessed April 19, 2019, https://countrymeters.info/en/United_states_of_america_(USA).

[67] Bob Skiles, "Would Cicero Consider Donald Trump a Traitor?", Research Gate .net, July 7, 2016, accessed April 30, 2019, https://www.researchgate.net/post/Would_Cicero_consider_Donald_Trump_a_traitor.

[65] Richard R. Beeman, Ph.D., "Perspectives on the Constitution: A Republic, If You Can Keep It," Constitution Center.org, accessed April 30, 2019, https://constitutioncenter.org/learn/educational-resources/historical-documents/perspectives-on-the-constitution-a-republic-if-you-can-keep-it

[66] Ketcham, Ralph. *The Anti-Federalist Papers and the Constitutional Convention Debates.* (New York: Signet Classic, 1986), 107.

[70] Rossiter, Clinton. *The Federalist Papers.* (New York: Signet Classic, 1961.), 81.

[71] Ibid.

[72] 1995 - July/August: In the CFR's Foreign Affairs, prominent CFR member Arthur Schlesinger, Jr. exclaims: "We are not going to achieve a new world order without paying for it in blood as well as in words and money." ARTHUR MEIER SCHLESINGER, JR

[73] "David Rockefeller", Wikipedia, accessed April 30, 2019, https://en.wikiquote.org/wiki/David_Rockefeller.

[74] 1974 Foreign Affairs Magazine Quote – unable to find

[75] Kissinger quote – unable to find[7]

[6] Brzezinski, Zbigniew K. *Between Two Ages: America's Role in the Technetronic Era.* (New York: Viking Press, 1970), 260.

[77] Deanna Spingola, "The New World Order, by Conquest or Consent? Part 1," Spignola.com, May 5, 2006, accessed April 23, 2019, http://www.spingola.com/new_world_order1.htm.

[78] David Rockefeller", Wikipedia, accessed April 30, 2019, https://en.wikiquote.org/wiki/David_Rockefeller.

[79] "The Times of London newspaper, opinion-editorial commentary, 1865", Liberty Tree.ca, accessed April 30, 2019, http://libertytree.ca/quotes/The.Times.of.London.Quote.573D.

[80] Deanna Spingola, "The New World Order, by Conquest or Consent? Part 1," Spignola.com, May 5, 2006, accessed April 23, 2019, http://www.spingola.com/new_world_order1.htm.

[81] Hitler quote – unable to find

[82] Garnett, Constance, translator. *The Brothers Karamazov.* By Fyodor Dostoyevsky. eBooks.Adelade.edu.au, December 27, 2014, accessed on April 28, 2019, https://ebooks.adelaide.edu.au/d/dostoyevsky/d72b/complete.html

[83] "Washington's Farewell Address to the People of the United States", govinfo.gov, accessed April 30, 2019, https://www.govinfo.gov/content/pkg/GPO-CDOC-106sdoc21/pdf/GPO-CDOC-106sdoc21.pdf

[84] "The Correspondence of Thomas Jefferson by Subject," Cooperative-Individualism.org, accessed April 27, 2019, http://www.cooperative-individualism.org/jefferson-thomas_correspondence-government-just-powers-1799.htm

[85] Income tax use for first time by Abe Lincoln 1861 tax was 3% on incomes above $800 per annum. Increased their time more ended in 1872. Acc. May 6 2020 Page 308 Dewey P.H.D. financial history U.S.. acc. May 7 2020.

[86] O.P.I.C. Overseas Private Investment Corp. Official website (http://www.o.p.i.c..gov.

[87] Spanish American War U.S. History Book Pg 15 Prentice Hall Inc. 1957 Acc. 5-7-2020.

[88] U.S. office management and budget. Census could not find bid.

[89] Ibid

[90] Ibid.

[91] U.N. Human Right 1948 Encyclopedia Page 102 Article 3-29 Acc. May 7 2020.

[92] Documents of American History #128 P 237 Niles Register Vol. XXV P137-138 Acc. June 5th, 2020

[93] Thomas Jefferson Government Fugal Ford Edition Volume 327 1899 Freedom Digest American Classic Page 80 Simplicity. acc. June 5, 2020.

[94] Democratic Socialist Party. acc. June 5, 2020.

95 Dictionary under Nazi. National Socialist German Workers Part. acc. June 5, 2020

Printed in the USA
CPSIA information can be obtained
at www.ICGtesting.com
LVHW092351200824
788829LV00029B/385